Martina Evan

NOW WE
CAN TALK
OPENLY
ABOUT
MEN

CARCANET

First published in Great Britain in 2018
by Carcanet Press Limited
Alliance House, 30 Cross Street
Manchester M2 7AQ

A CIP catalogue record for this book is available from
the British Library, ISBN 9781784105785.

The publisher acknowledges financial assistance
from Arts Council England.

An earlier version of the first eight monologues appeared
in *The Stinging Fly* 33:2 (Spring 2016). The author acknowledges
the invaluable support of The Royal Literary Fund.

This book would never have been written without
the inspiration & help of Louise Ryan in its
early stages twenty years ago.

Supported using public funding by
ARTS COUNCIL
ENGLAND

PART 1

Mrs Kitty Donavan
Mallow, 1919

page 9

PART 2

Miss Babe Cronin
Dublin, 1924

page 53

for Louise Ryan

PART ONE

MRS KITTY DONAVAN
MALLOW, 1919

1.

I was in a weakness. I couldn't stand up,
leant back against the wall like a drunkard.
Was that Himself I'd seen on the back
of a Crossley tender on Main Street?
The truck came down the hill & out
of the back appeared — a pair of red eyes.
They pinned me, bored me. It was an outrage.
A small Tan or maybe an Auxie, lounging
in the back against the canvas with a bayonet
pointed at my waist. The head off Himself
in a cracked leather coat with goggles
hanging round his neck. After twelve years.
Could he have clambered out the other
side of Sullivan's Quay that night in Cork
ran away fast with his bowler under
his arm? We never found the hat although
Eileen Murphy & myself searched high
& low, tearing the damp walls, our hands
bright green from the moss.

2.

Eileen Murphy was tough out. I should have
listened to her that night when she said
to shove his head down in the water with
my boot. I wanted him to be taken by God
with no hand in it at all myself but
of course that was a Sin of Omission
so I was a black sinner too. We should have
called the constabulary the minute
he slithered in. They say a drunkard
has more lives than a cat. Lurching up the road
every night, steamed to the gills, taking the two
sides of Blarney Street – horses & carts
the whole lot & not a hair of his head
damaged. His white collar shining in the green
gaslight. How many times did he fall down
& rise again like an India rubber ball?
& what was there to stop him rising
again? The body wasn't found & no one
saw Jesus rise on Easter Sunday either.
He is not here, for he has risen, as he said
he would. Come & see the place where he lay –
& that is the gospel according to Matthew.

3.

My brain wouldn't run straight in its track,
lurching & shooting red electric sparks
up the right side of my face. We'd a doing
from the Tans in June, the night of the attack
on Eileen but this was worse. Because staring
hurts worst of all. This fellow was morning-
sober not like the Tans who couldn't see
straight with the drink. One fellow held himself
up with his rifle, using it like a walking stick
to stop himself from falling down. Trying to
do the big man before Flora. The fellow
in charge leant up against the wall for balance,
left a green smear after him. I was scrubbing
for days. You never knew what way they'd turn.
A Tan might be sticking his head under
the hood of a baby's pram saying he couldn't
get over the blue eyes of the Irish,
next he'd be trying to *click* with a girl,
then you could turn a corner & a gang
of them would be stamping on an old man's hand.
People ran like chickens in front. Savage
drivers but expert. The tenders swept carts,
people & animals into the ditches –
pirate patches over their eyes, metal hooks
instead of hands slashing the air, gathering
leaves off the trees as they drove past. Dark
faces & stained fingers. The people said
they had come from hell & you could still smell
the singe off them. I couldn't smell the singe
only engine oil because they were pure out
of their minds about motors, couldn't stop
driving even for themselves. They got tangled
up with the Hounds of Duhallow out beyond

Burnfort on the Island Road & even the great
Britisher, Mrs Pound said she was angry
with Lloyd George for sending them because the
language out of them you wouldn't hear it
out of Turks. How lucky we were to have
the 17th Lancers, The Duke of Cambridge's
Own between us & the Cockney scum.

4.

The darting pain ran against the right side
of my face. If I could turn the clock back
to Thursday the first, I'd have got off my
chair faster & that was the cause – getting
frozen in a draft before the curfew
standing on top of my green painting chair,
pinning the vermilion blankets over
the window for the black-out with Scissors
Number 1 in my hand for protection.
A pure perishing mist rose up from under
the bridge while I stood foolishly too long,
with the scissors. The two rivers twining
& separating in my mind, a pair
of snakes – the Lee & the Blackwater – had I
left my husband underwater in Cork
only for him to resurrect himself in Mallow?

5.

Captain Galway, Auxiliary, was an
ex-officer with some very queer ideas
about whose side he was on. I didn't
know if he was a gentleman at all
& Mr Bloom hinted the same. Someone
told Eileen, she sent a fiery letter
from Dublin. I couldn't believe how
the news had shot through Royal Mail
so fast & Eileen was down toute suite on top
of me by letter, boiled up completely
about the two of them walking openly
in the streets of Mallow. Flora, in her
three-quarter-length smashed strawberry coat
& the Captain in mould-green, the empty
sleeve pinned to his epaulette. The whole town
killed from looking at them. Galway, blonde, too
handsome. People were scared of the Auxies
more than the Tans – their old eyes in their young
faces under their black Glengarry caps, ribbons
fluttering on their necks. They hung off
the side of the tenders, as mean as you like,
in rifle green. Constable Doon gave out
about Flora cutting her hair. A Woman's
Crowning Glory, he looked down over his long
moustache at the toes of his boots, standing
outside Broadview barracks. Well, that's the youth,
I said, walking away with my messages.
John Lucy's lamb chops were dripping blood out
of my basket – he'd given me a free
sheep's head as well with instructions how to
cook the head for a healthy mutton broth
because he thought Flora had fallen away.
The whole Town was telling me that after she
cut her hair.

6.

He appeared again on the Saturday
wearing brown boots laced up to his knees,
standing across the road from the house by
the Royal Red post box. Halfway through painting
the parlour cocoa with cream on the wainscot,
I threw open the window for the fumes
& saw him staring in with his hand on
His Majesty's mail. Small & neat like Himself,
only yellow, maybe he'd gone abroad
after his escape, couldn't he have fought on
the sands of Gallipoli? & the pain
was kneeing into my brain from the night
before, as if he had opened my head like
an egg & was spooning it out. If he
wasn't Himself then who was he? Was he
after Flora for espionage? &
for which side? Didn't Sinn Fein make the girls
spy for them? Eileen Murphy said they all
volunteered but young girls are easily forced.
I pulled my eyes away from him, cast them
right down to tongues of my brown button boots.
Mrs Pym's crimson dressing gown was thrown
across the sewing table half cut out
as I took to my bed with Wrixon's
linctus. The bottle stood on the table
by me, staining the broderie anglaise
brown in the dark. I couldn't move,
hardly able to breathe, my lungs shrunk
to the size of two teaspoons tied
around my throat.

7.

I'd just gone off, when the two of them
came back in & I had to get up again
out of my bed, wrap my sea-green shawl round
me, feel for my carmine slippers with heavy
lead feet. Go down, say good evening, pretend
that I was civilised towards him &
his mutilated arm. I didn't doubt
he'd a mutilated brain to go with it.
Not one of those fellows came back normal.
If Flora had a father, he would call
him in, demand a doctor's certificate
but what could I do? Flora went red every
time she spoke to him. I wondered if it
was me. Me, staring with my brown linctus
eyes. It is a hard fact that not one
of us can see ourselves from the outside.
But something was not right. He was handsome,
no one was in any doubt about that.
Not real gentry but not a shrivelled yoke
from the East End of London either.
One of them outside St Mary's church
on the Sunday, grinning over his bayonet
with his monkey face. His bandolier strapped
across his wrinkled olive jacket
& his thighs no wider than rolling pins
inside his black trousers. I couldn't bear
to look at him. The officer class
had the shoulders to carry the jackets –
a bunched uniform was always an affront
to my eyes because I was brought up
in tailoring with the highest respect
for the tailoring laws. Captain Galway
knew how to fill his uniform, apart

from the left sleeve & it was the empty
sleeve that had lured Flora. Sucked her up
like a hungry straw.

8.

I was only in the door from Mass
on Sunday when I thought I saw Himself
out the corner of my eye. I was afraid
to turn. I took Flora up to the top
of the house & she craned her eye against
the crack of the maroon velvet curtains.
Can you see anything? Her short shining hair
the colour of a camel-haired coat
over the delicate white bone of the knob
of her neck. Why couldn't she come home
from her typing job in the evenings, sit
quiet instead of drawing attention
to herself on the streets? Father Daly's
sermon had been red-hot. I had to fix
my eyes on the back of Mrs Bolster's moss-green skirt.
Afraid to look up though her hooks &
eyes were twisted & that was torture for me.
Father Daly said he was adding to
the Bishop's ex-communication order
& that he would have steps taken to see
women in Sinn Fein were taken out along
with the men. It's easy to see how Adam
committed Original Sin
with Eve beside him egging him on.
If such a woman came to the altar
for Holy Communion, he would walk past
her not to sully the Blessed Sacrament.

9.

Flora had great carriage, sitting upright
in the Indian Yellow dress I sewed
for her from the remnants of the silk dresses
I made for Mrs Cronin's fat triplets.
She didn't get the grace from me because
I was hunched up all my life from sewing.
I spoilt her. How could I help myself? No
kinder girl in Ireland. She couldn't even
bear for me to kill the lice on her head.
She had to walk out of the kitchen when
I prepared the sheep's head for the mutton
soup, singeing its eyebrows like John Lucy had
instructed. & I was disgusted too. Golly!
Flora talked like him, This is a rotten war.
That fellow was fragile. What brought him over
to Ireland? The ten shillings a day that
Lloyd George promised would be an expensive
ten shillings for Captain Galway. My bones
creaked with the knowledge every time I looked
at him. & I didn't care as long
as he didn't bring Flora down with him.
She was like a swan that people can't help
wanting to stone or maim. Eileen Murphy
forced Flora to the floor to rub the wart
of her knee against her nose but she never
succeeded in passing it on to her.
Flora's nose grew up perfect. Her face
was very small, as white as a button
mushroom under her camel-coloured hair,
hardly eating, giddy, talking about
the Captain, He's a socialist, you know!

10.

Mr Bloom was on the street, with the steam
coming off his navy coat. Mrs Bloom
had been taken away again after
gunmen broke into Annabella. His back
to the sign on the wall for shoe polish,
HALLO – IT CANNOT BE ECLIPSED!
He asked for Flora, how was her health now?
But I knew what he meant. The Captain is
a Socialist! I asked Mr Bloom what
did he think of that? He didn't answer.
His brown face reddened as he shook out
the *Cork Examiner* in front of me.
He said that it was no time for ideas
with RIC men shot every day, riots
in Tipperary & every Cork baker
on strike after the Great War allowed all
kinds of elements into the army.
He didn't mention Mrs Bloom but I
hoped she was safely locked up this time.

11.

I went up then to Lenihan's Drapers
& they took my sign for their front window.
I'd decorated it with crimson tulips
like I'd seen in the Blooms' conservatory,
the time I went to help them sedate her.
Irish hand-embroidered emerald voile
jumper very smartly cut, trimmed with heavy
embroidery & inserts of Irish lace
in three sizes. Two Tans were outside
Totty Byrne's tobacco shop, they had
Mick Burke, his face the colour of blood under
his foxy hair, up against the wall.
One of them going through his pockets,
the other, jaundiced under a fur hat,
smiled at me, said Mother! Was he hinting
about Flora? Or God, maybe Eileen?
If they knew our associations, they'd
be emptying petrol cans over the house
at midnight. Thank God the spot beside
the post box was empty but I thought
I heard whistling up on the roof. I took
the finest crochet hook & stuck it in
the side pocket of my housedress that
I might drive it through his yellow eyeball.

12.

Even the new potatoes were green-tinged.
I threw the sheep's head out for Bolsters' cat
& there were gangs of cats in the back yard
for several evenings. You could hear them
nanging into all the gristle & bone.
Flora said there was an Auxiliary friend
of Captain Galway's called Fuzzy Wuzz
because of the silver plate in his head.
Fuzzy Wuzz was always sent in when they
needed to have what they called Rough House
& Captain Galway didn't think it was fair.
Rough House, in God's name what is that? I asked.
& she said, You are always against him!
He's a socialist, she repeated. I asked
if socialism would be his answer for
St Peter at Heaven's gates. Flora flicked
through pattern books, her face carnation pink
& I thought that for all any of us knew,
Captain Galway might have a matching
silver plate in his own head.

13.

Too much of the elixir that evening
& the cats still nanging at the sheep's head.
I couldn't bear to look at them. I had
a cup of cocoa & Bolands' biscuits
for my supper before falling asleep
my head on the large fuchsia pincushion.
I woke up with dots all across my face.
I'd have taken more elixir only
for I'd have to ask Mr Wrixon
& that chemist was so fierce narrow-minded.
I should not rejoice over Mrs Bloom
but I hoped she would stay away this time.
I didn't know if I should order Flora
to stay inside. I tried to imagine
putting my boot down hard, I forbid you!
but I didn't seem to have it in me.
I checked in the yellow sewing basket
for weapons but it only had needles.
The green sewing basket was the best with
the seven scissors in descending sizes.

14.

Flora came in quietly so not to wake me
but didn't I spot her from the parlour
with her teal strapped shoes held in her hand.
I asked her about Captain Galway even though
he was the last person I cared about.
A sad fellow. I thought he was cruel
at first, the way his blonde hair was stretched tight
on his forehead by the Glengarry bonnet
& the cigarette stuck between his lips.
Now I had to hear all about his great
affection for horses, how he haunted
the Lancers' stables in the evenings,
patting the mares & the foals & so on.
& more sadness heaped on top of sadness –
horses dying in agony in the Great War.
When he was in the training camp in Wales,
the suffering of ponies going down
into the mines in cages, rolling their eyes,
never to have the sun again in their lives.
They didn't ask to go down, said Flora.
It was a brown & doleful evening &
I read aloud from *The Girl's Indoor Book* –
Make acquaintance with as many colours
as you please, but let the colours of your
choice, like the friends of your bosom, be a
select & well-tried few. I do not think
she heard a single word.

15.

I woke with tapping pain on the right side
of my head, like a woodpecker knocking
on a tree. I thought the lid would shoot off
my head like a saucepan under pressure.
I went out to the window but there was no
sign of Himself in the brown boots only
Dick Bolster in green-stained overalls letting
himself in next door. He looked up at me
as I drew back embarrassed. What a risk
he was taking outside in the curfew.
I supposed Mrs Bolster would be relieved
to have him inside. She was nice & quiet
just nodding at me over the clothesline when
our eyes met. No need for talk. The best kind
of neighbour. Constable Doon said that she
was a tasty dresser when she was young,
hard to believe with her twisted hooks & eyes
on Sunday morning. I used to think Doon
was a Molly, looking at women's clothes.
I found out after he was a G-man.
That was how he got his information.

16.

The next Sunday, Mass was more gruelling.
The majority of the congregation
had grasped the complete wrong end of the stick,
according to Father Daly. Women were
not put on earth to be happy but
to do good. Not to be dressing up,
cutting their hair or walking the streets
with foreign soldiers. Young girls, stay at home
like your mothers before you. Flora was red
& I am sure I was too. I had drawn
my hatpin at the wrong angle, the point
of the pin was piercing my brain. Vanity
is a terrible thing, women obsessed
with finery & reflections. Mirror,
mirror, on the wall, who is the fairest
of them all? He was roaring with his face
purple as a plum. As if we had time
for standing in front of the glass, asking
it questions. Ladies, it's the grave ye should
prepare for! That was well for him to say.
I wasn't dead yet & I had to make
my living. Mrs Fahey's fingers met
mine in the holy water afterwards.
Take no notice, said she, there was never
one who could cut a costume like yourself.
Thanks be to God, she asked me to run up
some tennis frocks for her three strong daughters.
We'll buy a chicken from John Lucy
on the strength of it, I said to Flora
but sure no sooner was my key in the door
when I saw the dire brown shape at the post box.

17.

& I after only getting my first relief
from the lid of the pain pressing down
on my head again. Can you see him too?
I was expecting Flora to say no
like she'd been saying last week but I was
about to get another land because
she said, Do you think he is off his chump?
I don't know, I said. I was hoping
he was all in my own imagination.
He didn't remind her of anyone, thanks
be to God, maybe he was some fellow
gone loony from the trenches. Unless,
of course, he was a pretender. Himself
was the most cunning blackguard of all,
his favourite pastime sowing discord
everywhere he went.

18.

Flora said Captain Galway was browned off.
I thought I'd distract her with a pattern book.
Imagine that on the chaise longue at Annabella!
I could never get over Mr Bloom's house,
its Greek columns, lawns down to the Blackwater.
Flora reddened, she asked me if I knew
Tans were murdering unarmed civilians
& I said of course I knew. The whole town knew
but we were all trying to soldier on.
Captain Galway was upsetting Flora.
He'd feigned sick to get out of being part
of an ambush near Burnfort. God, I said.
After the suspicion on us, after Eileen,
couldn't you have stayed away from trouble?
& she started crying & I felt like
a brute & kept breaking down myself
before I pulled myself up again &
made tea & we sat in the back kitchen
with our elbows sitting in the halves of
scooped out lemons to whiten them.

19.

The 14th was the anniversary.
That September day in 1908
we left Cork City for good. When we
stepped off the Dublin train that Sunday,
the silver tracks gave me the impression
it was the Blackwater river itself
flowing under our feet. We clittered
over the wooden boards of the railway bridge.
as Mr Bloom stepped out of the shadow.
The blackest eyes over his black moustache.
He picked up Flora, she was always light
even though she was eight & down we went
descending the hill of Ballydaheen
in the pony & trap, he rang the bell
by pressing his yellow boot to a button
on the floor of the trap. I was holding on
to the emerald veil of my hat.
I should have worn widow's black but Mallow
was like a foreign country to me where
I thought I'd never be recognised.
The military display was across from
the railway station outside the barracks –
the brass band playing, the instruments
blasting & blazing in the sun. Lancers
on horses, in red dress uniforms, the plumes
of white feathers bubbling in the wind like
fountains on top of the shining helmets.
Flora thought it was all for us.

20.

Then the man disappeared from the post box.
The ground around it was empty for days.
My scissors swam like a dolphin with relief.
I flew through tissue paper, cutting patterns.
I even put my hand on the red post box
like it was a friend who had come back to me.
When no one was looking. I was careful.
No one would do business with a mad woman.
I traced the crown & the letters of Royal Red.
Eileen Murphy said that we would have
our own post boxes soon, green ones instead of red.
I'd imagined something magnificent like
a pure Peacock hue until she showed me
the colour on a bachelor's gate
on the road to Quartertown. Pure disgusting.
A horrible dark green like an old leaf
of cabbage you'd see a snail on top of.

21.

Mrs Pound flamed after Father Daly's sermon.
After the work you did on his old altar
cloth, how dare that man fumble with a Lady's
livelihood. Mirror, mirror, he should look
at himself – the tub of guts! & she ordered
four quilted satin dressing gowns, aquamarine,
royal purple, geranium & heliotrope.
She should have stayed away from loud colours
with the size she was but who was I to bite
her golden hand? Flora & myself could
hardly squeeze into the parlour with all
the materials. Flora was a slow worker
but exquisite. I never saw tiny stitches
so straight. She double-worked every hem
& stroked the gathers while I wrestled with
the armholes, Mrs Pound had a queer shape –
none of the dummies were right for her.
If I had the room I'd have bought a fourth one,
it would have been worth it.

22.

There was rivalry there between Eileen
& Flora over the sewing. Eileen was old,
nearly twelve when she started the lessons.
It was the nuns that asked me & I was glad
to help the creature when her mother died
& she came in from Glen. I had to start her
at the bottom rung. I suppose she found
it hard, doing run & fell on a piece
of stiff Bolton sheeting with Flora ahead
on embroidery & double crewel.
Eileen said afterwards that it was worthwhile
because she was the fastest darner of socks
in the IRA flying column. It killed
me to hear it but she had no pity.

23.

The nuns wanted Eileen out of that farm
when her mother died. Sister Lorenzo came
& asked me if it was too late to teach
Eileen my trade. It was only the three
brothers on the farm, rebels to their centre
bones, in a hovel without a single
item of grace not even a tablecloth
to throw across the old crooked table.
Cissy Young coming in to boil their spuds.
John, Jimmy, Jacky, I didn't care what
their names were, they were too dirty altogether,
their trousers held with grey twine. Flora liked
going out there – the fairy ring, the stream, shining
stones. I never saw these beauties, only
a bleak bare place with lonely blackthorn bushes.
But I thought the country air was supposed
to put peaches into the skin of girls.
Cissie Young was hard to look at, brown face
like a wrinkled fist on her strong neck with
a man's suit jacket over a raggedy
old skirt & she chewing a pipe. I thought
she might be mad that I'd taken Eileen
out of the place. Hell leow, she said to me
in a queer accent like she was pretending
to be English when she met me on Main Street.

24.

Have you been here before? Cissie Young asked
Flora & I thought Cissie was praising
her brains until Eileen, God forgive her,
said that Cissie thought Flora might be
a changeling. The only way to be sure
someone wasn't a changeling was to
challenge them with fire or iron.
Flora never told me about that part
or that Cissie Young was taking me off
in the kitchen, throwing shapes to show
how I used to be walking up & down
the town like a snob, straight as an arrow,
putting on an English accent. She said that
I went into Totty Byrne's & said Hawf
a pound of chocolate creams in an English
accent. Eileen told me this, laughing &
I said that I said no such thing. I had
a strong Cork City accent my whole life,
if I was whipped, you couldn't cut it out
of me. Cissie said only the fairies
have fair hair & brown eyes so Flora must
be one. They told Flora about a fairy,
a bad yoke that lived in Murphy's cottage
fifty years before. Big long teeth on her,
slipping over her lower lip & she only
had to look at a joint of meat &
it would be crawling with worms before nightfall.
That Ould Murphy had to drive an iron
fork through the yoke before his own daughter
was restored to him. Flora was seventeen
before she could tell me. A crown of thorns
to think she suffered alone every night
rather than upset me. & that was the thanks

I got for sending a bag of expensive
brown bananas that Mr Bloom gave us
to that pair of thundering blackguards.

25.

Eileen said that she was only hardening
Flora up because I was too feeble
to do it. I am not feeble, I said.
Does giving a girl a wart on the end
of her nose harden her up? The arguments
raged between us & about politics
too. I was no fool of a Britisher.
I'd seen low-down British soldiers whipping
fellows with their own belts down Cork alleys
but half of them were Irish themselves
so we were always mixed-up and confused.
Who likes to be in thrall to another power?
With armed policemen? No thank you but
I did not want to die for Ireland either.
I had to make my living. Eileen laughed,
Sure isn't it only the greatest calling?
She'd talk of the plantation of Munster
& cursing Ould Spenser, writing poetry
in the evening after clearing the Irish
like nettles by day. The young girls hung
by the neck with their long hair, the corpses
held as examples against the walls
of Cork City. She was always morbid
& with brothers like that, there was no hope
for her.

26.

One Murphy brother left by '22
& he not speaking to Eileen because
they took opposite sides in the Civil War.
Pieces of her hair were blowing everywhere
after the Tans left that night. The brothers
safe in their dug-out, only for Cissy
tying up Eileen's hand she'd have bled
to death. Maybe Cissy's old pishogues worked.
Her mother was a known witch who could bring
people out in black boils or throw a wisp
of madness in their eyes. During the attack
on Eileen, we had more Tans down on us
& Flora stood up too, Leave my mother
alone! With all her shyness she was braver
than a lot of them. But the Tans couldn't see
straight & when I took down the big bottle
of Holy Water to give us strength, they thought
it was whiskey & rushed forward fast.
Maybe it was feeling foolish that got them
out of the house or they just had to quench
their undying thirst. They were in complete awe
of the fine clothes hanging in the parlour.
Like Oxford Street, one of them said, his arm
around the fattest dummy.

27.

Captain Galway looked shook the next evening
when he came in with Flora. I was ready
for black-out before sunset & the sun
pouring through the vermilion blankets
turned our three faces red. The piece of chalk
was in my hand, I was marking a length
of green paisley. I had to put it down
because of the fierce tremor he gave me.
His eyes were huge black discs, like I don't
know what, maybe an Egyptian dug up
out of a tomb would have queer eyes like that.
Flora was smiling with a glaze over
her own eyes. Or maybe it was the tears
in my own. Do you believe in torture?
he said & electric sparks crawled right across
my cheek. I picked up Scissors No. 4
beside my leg & turned round to Flora
to see what she thought. He's going to write
to the Government, she said as she rolled
thimbles right across the green paisley,
not looking me in the face. I knew then
in that moment, he was drugged right up with
I didn't know what & his head was just
a black hole with the pupils of his eyes
dead tunnels leading to the underground.

28.

Why did the Captain think he was paid
ten shillings a day? Wasn't it only
to be a brute? But he was too fragile.
I came out in a sweat when Flora told
me she'd told him about Eileen – the knock
on the cottage door, someone whispering, Miss!
Miss Murphy! Eileen, rushing to open.
That awful lonesome place & three men
in black masks. Clouds over the moon
as they pulled her to the well on her face
by the waves of her black hair. One of them
stepping right up on her back to cut it off.
Another was stooped over with the razor
still in his hand when she pulled off the mask,
I'll identify you in court! Eileen rash,
to the last breath & he only grabbed the hand
that pulled the mask, cut it in two between
the two middle fingers up to the wrist.
She would have died only for Cissy Young.

29.

What good did Flora do telling all that
to Captain Galway? He was confused enough,
drinking his tea, his shaky hand lighting
one long cigarette after another.
There was a green aspect to his face
that I didn't like. I was wondering
if I should throw a mad fit to get him
out of the house because he wasn't safe
& what curse was upon myself & Flora,
minding our own business sewing away
like two good creatures, going to Mass,
keeping the house clean? First Eileen & now
him dragging us into a red-eyed storm.

30.

I'd have sent him away if I wasn't
afraid of what he or Flora might do
in their self-righteous state. After my first
sup of tea, pain shot through my teeth
& my lips went pure numb. The two
must have thought I was making faces at them.
I went up the stairs & opened my brown
bottle, sitting on the side of my apple-
green bed. After four spoons, I went over
to the window, holding my head at an angle
to reassure myself that he wasn't
there but he was. Looking more like Himself
than ever & wearing a big fur hat.
Even with my ruined eyesight I saw
from the direction of his head
he was looking at Bolsters' just as Dick
Bolster came up the street as pale as cream
in his painting overalls with a ladder
on his shoulder. Dick nodded at Himself
laid down his ladder, put a match
to his cigarette & the red tip danced
like a fly in the blackness. I drew back.
Four spoons from the bottle, four more
before I slept.

31.

I was out along the Navigation Road
on my way to a fitting for Mrs Nagle.
The crab apples squashed flat into the road
were in pink & white rounds like fancy cakes.
I didn't see the Lancers on their horses
at first. I had my head down, measuring
Mrs N. in my mind. I could have dressed
her from morning to night & not charged her
a penny because it was like fitting
a goddess. I was making her a gown
of georgette carried out in two shades, flame
& grey & the bodice trimmed with heavy
embroidery, the same grey as the skirt
& the next thing I was looking into
the big chest of a prancing strawberry roan.
A stocky fellow with hunter green eyes
and a black handlebar moustache spoke but
I could not hear him over the sudden din
of hooves as he tipped the peak of his hat
& pulled the horse sideways, very elegant.
Some fellow on the other side to me
was calling hup, hup & in the frozen
moment, the laying down of horses came
into my head. I'd never seen it done but
I'd heard Mr Bloom telling how he saw
the Lancers getting the horses to kneel
while they were still sitting on their backs.
He saw them on the Portobello Beach
when Queen Victoria was still alive
but when I looked again, the Lancers were
gone, hooves clopping away down the road.

32.

It was a different kettle of fish
on Main Street with Tans blowing cigarette
smoke in people's eyes. I kept my eyes on
the ground when I saw two brown lace-up boots
coming at me. I turned into Cronin's
window pretending to be looking at the
wren hat she had on the display. The boots
marched on as I stared at the veil, my eyes
strained & blurred so I nearly staggered when
I turned around & saw Galway standing
outside of Totty Byrne's tobacco shop,
a lit cigarette between his lips
& the Glengarry cap pulled tight, in front
of a sign for SPINET SMOKING MIXTURE.
Mr Bloom came round the corner, dark
& damp-looking as always, in his navy
pullover & waders. He stopped. Galway
seemed to twitch as they spoke. Mr Bloom
pulled out a pipe & the two of them stood
in the curls of blue smoke. They didn't see me.
I passed on like a ghost.

33.

Once Mrs Bloom stopped her bottle-green
motor in the Main Street, mortifying me.
She said she was having sherry trifle
made for Mr Bloom. She was tiny &
I'd always admired her mauve costumes
& mauve suede shoes so it was an awful shock
to smell the whiskey waves & hear her say
that the trifle was going to be whipped hard.
I suppose she meant me but sure, I was
as innocent as snow. He visited me
only the once in the parlour. I was
so mesmerised, I didn't notice my ankles
up against the red-hot fire screen until
I smelt the scorch. He spoke about Mallow,
a spa town in its day – an Irish Bath with
Henry Grattan coming down & having
his chocolate in The Long Room with balls,
Ridottos & the Rakes of Mallow dancing
minuets. & when the Lancers weren't
dancing, they would challenge a fellow
to a duel at the drop of a hat.

34.

All I asked Flora was to lie low but
that went out the window too. I was
afraid to look. I was afraid to post
a letter to Eileen. Himself was gone again
but I couldn't pretend he'd never been.
Then Flora was home late for her Bovril.
The 28th September. She ran
up to her room when she came home from work.
It took me a good few minutes to get
after her, my breath had got so tight on
the stairs. I stood at the door, thin fingers
of Genoa cake on the china plate &
still she wouldn't be moved. She sat up still,
her back to the window & the best flame
coloured towel over her face & head –
like an Indian bride. She was crying
underneath without the smallest sound.
When Mr Sullivan came to the door –
only then was she persuaded downstairs.
He'd stood back by the post box to look up
at the house after knocking. It made me jump
when I saw his pose & I had to explain
that he reminded me of a man from
years ago who was believed to be drowned.

35.

The present is what's concerning us, Mr Barry
Sullivan's face was shining with the sweat
but he got her to come out from under
the towel & talk. The first Flora knew
about a shooting was when Captain Galway
passed her outside St Mary's & his face
was Mars red. She went up to him but he
only gave her a blonde push, shouted Shinner!
I said, Shooting! What shooting? & Mr Barry
Sullivan said that a Sergeant Gibbs was
shot in the stomach by the IRA
while he was shoeing a horse. Flora's eyes
streamed, They were all calling him Fuzzy Wuzz!
& I said, But wasn't Fuzzy Wuzz his friend?
Flora was only uncontrollable
again & I nearly put the towel
over my own head when Mr Sullivan
said but Captain Galway *is* Fuzzy Wuzz
& God, I wish we could all pity him
if we could but we can't.

36.

No one in town could breathe with it.
Sergeant Gibb's stomach bleeding out every
minute of the afternoon. The Canon
& the Protestant minister went up
to beg Colonel Peck for no reprisals,
surely be to God it wasn't Mallow's fault
that the other fellows stole the arms
when the Lancers were out exercising?
Weren't they only stranger blackguards
that blew in but after they blew out again,
in their motor, with a brazen fellow sitting up
behind playing the melodeon, it was Mallow
got the blame.

37.

I went out near four & every shop
was putting up shutters, nailing up zinc.
John Lucy thrust the chops into my gloved
hands telling me to run home quick because
the promise to the Canon was no good
after an aeroplane dropped a message
over the Barracks & flew to Buttevant
& Fermoy – troops were driving in
already & the Buffs from Lismore, too.
The trucks roared, changing gears at the top
of the town. Sulky fellows on the street,
pushing people, you would hardly recognise
them as Lancers & the man with the black
moustache was there, tapping the pavement
with his boot, holding the strawberry roan by
her bridle. Then like a vision, I saw
the small man in the brown boots whispering
to Miles Galway whose face was full of blood.
I was so sure it was Himself, pressure
rose in my own head. Captain Galway
looked at me & as Himself slowly turned
his head, I thought I could hear the leather
of his hat creaking. Sparks rose from my lips
bolts ran in through my ear & I ran fast,
leaving red spots from the chops on the ground.

38.

They lit everything, the creamery, the bank,
everything was flaming. They fired bottles filled
with petrol into any house with a light.
But I only heard that afterwards. Lying
in the cold, hearing the shouts & the bad
language outside was just beyond all.
They drove nails into every holy picture,
I heard that afterwards too. I was afraid
to even wash my hands & they were still
red from when I put the chops in the safe.
I could smell the blood the whole time, couldn't
go upstairs for the bottle of linctus
even when my head was shooting cannons
because I was sure we'd be called on
to do something. I put my green sewing
basket on my lap, gave out the rosary
which wasn't a bit like me.

39.

Just before midnight, the knock came. The Tan
with the yellow face although we couldn't
see it because we had the hallstand up
against the door. We were kneeling behind.
I had the jade rosary beads still twined round
my fingers. Even when he said he was sent
by Mr Bloom, still we wouldn't believe him.
He shouted through the keyhole, Quick! Smart!
pounding the door with the butt of his rifle.
When he roared out that Bolsters' was alight,
I said I would come out. He was a desperate
low-looking fellow, his eyes ringed in red
in his yellow face. We couldn't make out
a word of Cockney. Only when he pointed
with his yellow hands, did we know we were
to go to the boat & he rowed across
the Blackwater because Mr Bloom's poor hand
was in a sling after he tried to stop
the Lancers burning down the creamery
& the side of his face was reddened too.
I couldn't bring myself to look at him with
his green herringbone all singed & blackened.
That Tan cut the water like an arrow,
he must have been a boatman in his other
life. & that was it, in a blink we were
gone for good from Ballydaheen.

Part Two

MISS BABE CRONIN
DUBLIN, 1924

1.

It was very bad breeding from the word go.
Mrs Donavan was only adopted.
Twelve when an old tailoring couple took
her out of the nuns. There must have been bad
elements in her own family because
when Eileen got in trouble in '20,
Mrs Donavan cast her off. Put her
on the train from Mallow with five shillings.
Cool as cucumber. A young girl like that
with her hand cut in half but Eileen would
never hear a word against Aunt Kitty.
And Mrs Donavan was no lady.
She ended up as housekeeper to a Turk
in Mallow during the Troubles when the two
of them took steps to get his first wife locked up.
The wife met *him* when she was out foreign
& then he ended up with the property.
Black hearts. Blackguards.

2.

They said Eileen Murphy joined a convent
or she emigrated or died trying
to swim the English channel. She did not.
She did not die either with her own head
in a gas oven in Bermondsey &
she wasn't thrown off by a black & white
stallion. Pure lies. The girl is dead not
by her own hand. God Bless the Mark tonight.
She was thirty-one years of age, she had
the Blessed Sacraments & the priest at
the end. I was there & she was fit
to meet her maker.

3.

I met her first in Hayes's Hotel.
June '20. It was there I came again
when I was seeking her in '24.
I left Dublin for London for good
but I had to come back because of no
decent work in England for respectable
Irish stenographers. I found out, too
that the English are as bad as ourselves
& I could not make my way around.
I shake at the memory of entering
the soot-black mouth of the Underground.
But mostly I came back to see Eileen.
I was missing her something desperate
only when I returned to Hayes's again
the second time, she was gone.

4.

She disturbed the quiet home I had at Hayes's
when she arrived first in 1920.
I could hardly move my jaw, it was stiff
with the rage. The indignity of having
to listen to her whether I liked it
or not. Me. Who had no time for rebels.
An open tap of propaganda poured
out of her mouth from the minute she came
down to breakfast wearing men's grey breeches
& it was never turned off until
she was asleep. When I first saw her eyes
closed in the sitting room chair & making
no faces, I could see she was nice looking
in spite of the man's black cap, the cropped hair,
bitten nails, weather beaten face & all.
I put my silver-grey shawl over her.
The only good thing, crocheted by myself.

5.

& after I covered her with the shawl,
she stopped shrieking at me & we started
talking every night in the sitting room.
She showed me how to play cards. 45.
The highest in red & lowest in black.
A Cork game, very quick, she called the Jacks
Knaves. She told me about Mrs Donavan
& her sewing & the embroidery.
The seven sewing baskets & the three
dressmaking dummies, lined up like the three bears.
Mrs Donavan had five screens with swans
on them & eleven silk dressing gowns.
She got the customers to order more
material than they needed so she could
dress herself & the daughter for nothing.
Every night they sat with their elbows in the
halves of lemons to whiten them like they
were two Queen Cleopatras in the asses' milk.
I never said a word against those callous
blackguards to Eileen even though often I had
to nearly bite my tongue in two.

6.

After London, I spent two evenings drinking
black coffee out of white cups inside of
Mrs Hayes's office, my heart rising
with each hot sip in the hope that Eileen's
name would come up. But she spoke to me like
I was any old customer to plámás.
Pretending to be asking about coffee
houses in Oxford Street, Wouldn't I love
selling coffee & cream puffs instead of
being tied here to the bar & hotel.
She gripped me with the forks of her fingers,
Eileen put the whole hotel in danger –
the Freestaters were ready to light the torch.
Mrs Hayes cast a huge shadow behind her
& my own black shadow joined it so that
it looked like we were knocking our two heads
together. The clacking sound of her black
wooden buttons made my teeth clamp. I had
to ask her for hot whiskey for my cough
because she was holding out on me on
purpose. After two good swallows, I asked her
straight out. Where was Eileen gone? Oh God,
that's what everyone wants to know & it's
all politics & gossip. I said she
knew well that I was not interested
in gossip or politics but she bared her
false white teeth at me, God wouldn't I love
to know myself! I asked again even though
I knew she was against me. My stomach
was sinking, like feet in a marsh. When she
lowered the gaslight, our heads melted into
one giant shadow like the crown of a tree.

7.

Mrs Hayes & me were great at the word go
before Eileen came – when I was the pet.
My table napkin was in a stiff triangle
every morning by my white china egg cup.
Nelly brought in everything piping &
perfect. Nelly had a head of fierce curls
the colour of rain with small eyes to match.
The curls were twisted into a tight knob
in the morning, they'd spring out one by one –
she would have a head of small snakes on her
when she went to bed with her cocoa at ten.
Mrs Hayes said Nelly was desperate
for politics, never say nothing
against De Valera, he's Nelly's friend.
Then one June morning, eating my perfect
egg, looking out the window, I saw
Eileen playing with Marcel, the grey cat,
among the pots of white geraniums.
Noble Soldier, she was calling him &
pouncing around in white jodhpurs, a broom
on her shoulder, pretending to be doing
military manoeuvres. I thought she was
touched. & I was annoyed too because
the egg went cold while I was looking at her.

8.

We weren't friends too long, before Eileen
asked me to pick up a bag at a church
in the city centre. A fair-haired girl with
plaits down to her waist handed it over
but when she smiled at me, weren't her two
front teeth missing? In that church with the girl
dressed all in white among the white candles,
it was an awful shock to see her gums.
As if the door of hell opened, roared at me.
The minute I took the black bag, I knew
full well it was a firearm & I did not
waste time, only threw it in the Liffey.
When I faced Eileen afterwards, I told her
I didn't care what she said. I told her
so in black & white. I could be executed
on the spot for possession of a gun.
I saw street executions for myself,
saw a man pour blood over another
man's black patent shoes, running away down
the street shouting some cracked words in Irish.
I had no interest in that language.
I thought it was only a racket.

9.

But when I came back & she was missing,
I nearly went to Irish classes myself.
I would have done anything & they all knew
in the hotel that I was demented,
searching every day, going through savings
like water. Cantwell, the traveller squeezed
my shoulder & winked at me, asking me
if I'd heard anything from Eileen & that
seemed improper but grey & slippery
too though I couldn't pin-point what it was
he was hinting. His old teeth like black sticks
stuck out in a row at me. Maybe Eileen
was a bad girl really, making me carry
a gun. I could have been executed or
excommunicated. But I could never
think she was completely bad because she
wasn't a pretender.

10.

The girls at the office thought I was living
the sophisticated life. They implied
that it was slim flappers & Craven A
cigarettes at Hayes's Hotel unless
they were playing games with me of course &
it wouldn't be the first time. Maybe they
knew about the crowds of country men in
bad suits, their hair in oiled waves drinking
Guinness, bawling, roaring *The Foggy Dew*.
Mrs winking at me behind their backs
& winking at them behind my back.
One day she even winked at Marcel the cat.
I didn't imagine it. I saw her
at her tricks & winks in the big Jameson
whiskey mirror. Not at the beginning,
only when I got friendly with Eileen.

11.

I could never meet the right people.
The man in charge of our division, Smith,
a black Protestant, always kept me back.
A country girl like me, it would be nice
to be invited to people's houses, to have
a social life. But it was not to be.
When I became friends with Eileen Murphy,
Smith let on I was a Communist.
He was only looking for an excuse.
I always was & will be an outsider.
Eileen Murphy knew sophisticated
women though, women with plenty money,
leisure to get mixed up in politics.
They loaned her the jodhpurs & the puttees
& the fishermen pullovers. I should
have joined Sinn Fein, to meet the Right People.
Everyone was fired up about Freedom first.
But money is what gives you freedom.
Money, & I was always short of it.

12.

I never meant to stay at the hotel.
It was temporary but the Troubles started,
& you wouldn't know what or who was safe.
The rooms were always warm, no matter what
freezing fog gathered outside. I had the attention,
hot water, bedroom fires blazing away
bed starched, spotlessly clean & aired, heated.
During the Troubles, when I took my life
in my hands every morning, swinging out
the revolving doors to go to the Castle,
the Paradise continued. Nelly went
up & down with the boiling water &
the coal & the ashes & then Mrs Hayes
ironed my blouse. My white collar & cuffs
shone inside the blackness of the wardrobe.
I didn't know what Mrs Hayes saw in me.
Eileen Murphy said that Mrs Hayes thought
I was brainy, she liked having a guest
who worked at Dublin Castle. That might
be right, but it all went in the end &
my bed was pure icy.

13.

I want to make this point clear from the word go,
Mrs Hayes said to me my first night
in the hotel, I don't believe in politics.
She'd noticed my cough straight away
had me sitting in two minutes in front
of a boiling whiskey. Let those fumes through
the nose & down into your throat. They'll loose
everything. She picked up the glass, sniffed herself.
I've had a bellyful. I saw my family
starve because of politics. Fenians on the run
got more food in my mother's house than any
of us small children saw in the whole year.
Mrs Hayes was saying what I thought too.
Sinn Fein were only all about themselves.
Ourselves Alone. They named themselves well but
you had to be careful expressing views.
You could have the head snapped off you or worse.
Mrs Hayes & myself were great then.
Once a week, the Aladdin lamp came out
from behind the bar & she washed all her
ornaments, us chatting away, Marcel
between us with his grey chest out proud.
She had a pile of ornaments. A brass
map of Ireland bolted to a streaky
piece of mahogany, the three heavy brass
monkeys covering their eyes, ears & mouth.

14.

Mrs Hayes said to me she wondered if
she should have taken Eileen in at all.
Mrs Donavan didn't give her much choice,
sending Eileen by train like a parcel.
No one knew how bitter things were going
to get. Did we dream there would be Civil
War with the Freestate soldiers borrowing arms
from the British to gun down their comrades
of the week before? People were in shock.
Dublin was desperate. Records destroyed
in the Four Courts, the unvarnished truth
in black & white, our duty to preserve.
Eileen was involved in that. Herself &
the Irregulars. & everyone had enough
of them except for themselves. & maybe
they had enough of themselves too but were
too proud to admit it. Mrs Hayes raised
her voice only once & that was when
Eileen mentioned Men of Action. Action!
says Mrs Hayes. The same fellas would knock
you in their rush to get under the table
if they heard a shot two miles away.
Oh then, to hear them singing every night
Glorio, Glorio & Mother Ireland.
Mother Ireland must be sick to her stomach.

15.

After Mrs Hayes roared, Eileen ran off.
I never saw her do a tap apart
from feeding Marcel & combing his hair.
You couldn't control her, said Mrs Hayes
before she made me have a hot whiskey.
She was great if you were sick, she would force
you to take your medicine however hard
you protested. Eileen never took a drink –
she was that kind of fanatic – only
white lemonade. She slept in the attic
so she wouldn't keep us awake with her
own bad cough. A small room at the very top,
low ceiling with black beams & white tissue
paper wrapped over the naked light bulb.

16.

Eileen's brother wasn't talking to her
by the time of the second war, by then
both of the older brothers were shot.
On top of that, Mrs Donavan stopped
writing to her for a long time because
she said a man was watching their post box.
I don't know how Eileen swallowed that one.
Then Mrs Donavan was a live-in
housekeeper to the Turk, the young Flora
living with her, too busy for anything.
Mrs Hayes had to keep Eileen because
she had nowhere to go. But Mrs Hayes
did care a bit. She was mad when Eileen
went on the fast in Kilmainham with the rest
of the Cumann na mBan in '23.
A girl with a bad chest like that! She said
they were a right pack of users.

17.

Mrs Hayes was happy as long as
I had the cold shoulder against Eileen.
A bit of time to ourselves, Mrs Hayes
poured whisky & I could never bear waste
of any kind so I drank it down gratefully.
The sideways looks started after Eileen
& myself became friends. Her talk began
draining me then. There was no end to it.
Her business sense. Her old uncle, Sickly Dan
who always wore a slate-grey pinstriped suit
with shoes to match, could add up numbers
like a machine & looked down on rebels.
She agreed with him that John Redmond
was a gentleman that they stabbed in the back.
Stabbed by cowards hiding under women's
beds during the Troubles, the same fellows
who moved through the countryside fearless
in flying columns according to Eileen.
She's my own niece said Mrs Hayes but she's
an awful fool.

18.

I was getting close to Eileen Murphy
when she gave me the gun but we were out
again when I threw it into the river.
& then we were back together after
we got the joint fit of laughing during
John McCormack on the gramophone.
Mrs Hayes fingering her black wooden
buttons, eyeing at the whiskey mirror,
moving her lips to the long stream of words
pouring out, I hear you calling me. You
called me when the moon had veiled her light,
before I went from you into the night.
I came, do you remember? That night
Eileen told me about the black masked Tan
on her back, the razor, the rest of them
cheering him on. The neighbour tying her hand,
another masked man walking up & down
the boreen all night playing the mouth organ
to stop them going for the doctor.
I held her hand. Sure, what else could I do?
Smooth as silk along the scar, the rest as
rough as Marcel's tongue. Mrs Hayes came in
& looked hard at us. Eileen didn't see
because she looking down at the ground
but I could make out Mrs Hayes's cauliflower
shadow like the writing on the wall.

19.

Take it easy, says Mrs Hayes on the stairs.
I am going easy, I said but the truth
is I lost my head & I stopped being
the Best Guest in the Twenty-Six Counties.
It was very gradual at first but towards
the end, I would have to ask for my hot
water jar. The icy bed, as I said,
& whiskey never flowed freely after.
I was forced to buy it when I had a cold.
& I've had a cold from that day to this.
Sometimes Mrs Hayes would give me a dig,
ask me if I still considered myself
a great keeper of the Temperance Pledge.
A person has to take his medicine,
I said & You're right, too, says Mrs Hayes,
not meaning a word of it & making
sure I knew it with her bad tone.

20.

I was never able to take anything easy.
I delivered dispatches for Eileen. I met
dowdy black widows in churches, young
flappers in cream lace at lectures. I sat
up all night in the resident's lounge &
asked her to explain to me The Spanish
Armada & Hugh Dubh O'Neill's defence
of Clonmel. I never held her hand again
but I wanted to. I was 50 years
& Mrs Hayes thought I was an old fool.
Eileen didn't tell me where she went
or what she was doing. I was jealous of that.
I was jealous of the Vicks ointment that
Mrs Hayes told her to rub into her chest.
I wanted to do that. I wanted to sleep
in the attic too, under the picture
of Cathleen Ni Houlihan, under the
electric bulb in wispy white paper,
with the wooden picture puzzle that was
in the shape of a thirty-two county
map of Ireland.

21.

I questioned her too much & she would turn
away annoyed. Then I stopped the questions but
I would see her whispering with Mrs Hayes
& Nelly. I was sure that Nelly was
doing things for her. Hadn't Mrs Hayes
said Nelly was pure mad for politics?
Sometimes I'd break into a run after
I saw the edge of Eileen's grey pullover
revolving through the doors of the hotel but
when I got inside, the black & white tiled
hall would be empty & Nelly standing
there, with her rainy eyes, her head of snakes,
polishing the floor with her black boot wrapped
in a silver cloth. Eileen never asked
any more favours of me. I pretended that
was my doing. Mrs Hayes started giving
the odd hot whiskey again to encourage
me in the right direction. I worked late.

22.

I was coming home from Dublin Castle
looking forward to Mrs Hayes's chicken
mentioned in the morning. I tried not to
think of the ghosts as I crossed the yard.
Eileen said the great heroes & martyrs
like Emmet, O'Connell & Parnell
walked around Dublin, looking over
our shoulders to see what we were doing.
I felt agitated – a premonition
as I went through the revolving doors quick,
arriving on to the black & white tiles
of the foyer, dizzy to Mrs Hayes
twisting her rope of Woolworth's imitation
pearls & I thought she was going to choke.
I nearly choked myself
when I saw what was before me standing
on the mahogany stairs. Eileen with a
dark young fellow wearing a bandolier,
they were like two Napoleons posing.
Eileen pointing the gun first at Mrs Hayes
& then me. I'm taking him upstairs,
she was holding his hand. My stomach lurching
with the indecency of it. He was proud
& wild-looking like a horse – with a wine
birthmark on the lower half of his face
& neck. They ran up the stairs & Marcel
ran past them with his two eyes out on stalks.
All I wanted was to have great dignity
that no one would know the agitation
inside my grey costume only Mrs Hayes
sent me straight up after them, insisting
that Eileen would listen to no one but me.

23.

Mrs Hayes only wanted to keep her
hands clean of course with two soldiers
shot dead at Beggar's Bush barracks.
She knew well that Donnacha was mixed up
in it when Eileen took him by the hand.
Donnacha. The name would make Marcel laugh.
Half of those fellows had ordinary names
like John-Jo & Paddy five years before.
Now it was the fashion to wear some queer
old Irish name with your bandolier
& to hide under girls' beds. Mrs Hayes
was beside herself, tearing the black
buttons on her cardigan but she never
mentioned Beggar's Bush. Isn't she
after being just caught painting slogans
on the wall of the Dental Hospital
behind Trinity College? & she's after
threatening a Guard with her revolver?
I said I would rather be boiled in oil
than go after them only Mrs Hayes
said it was a matter of life or death.
Quick, quick! pushing her advantage. Before
Mr Cantwell & the other travellers
come back from the Freemasons. If Mr Cantwell
sees her he'll have the Civic Guards in. Quick,
quick, Miss Cronin. We're depending on you.

24.

What does it matter who he is? says she.
Only get him out of Hayes's hotel.
That pair doesn't care who he takes with him.
Mrs Hayes leaned at me in her black widow
skirt. He was in a shootout before
& shot an elderly aunt through the chin.
He is dynamite. She gripped my elbow,
Eileen is after injuring a Civil Guard.
Up I went & I shamed to be there
in that room under the white tissue paper.
She was zipping him into her ugly
moleskin skirt, pulling a lady's hat brim
down over his birthmark. He couldn't have
been more than seventeen. Eileen said
he had shot two Freestate soldiers at Beggar's Bush,
he would hang if I didn't help them.

25.

They stood at the open casement window,
looking at the roof. Eileen was shivering
in her sailor's jacket, her black hair blowing
into her eyes. I have a premonition,
I said. Don't go up on that roof.
I was remembering Jack Neville who
fell off a roof during the Troubles &
got impaled on street railings. Well, take him
out the front door, you so then, said Eileen
& like an eoinseach, I went down the stairs
with Donnacha. The Guard was in the hall,
looking right up at us, pretending, chatting
about Limerick. Mrs Hayes saying wasn't
it great that the Guard was from the County
Limerick too, like myself. & he was
nodding his head, saying that Limerick
people were great for a laugh. The biggest
sourpuss was myself as they knew full well.
Donnacha's arm trembling inside of my own.

26.

I gripped tighter to steady our landing
on the black & white tiles of the hall
which were blinding me something desperate.
The Guard must laughed at us inside himself.
Pretending to be girls out for the night.
I didn't even know where I was supposed
to be going if I was asked. Yes, lovely,
County Limerick, I said. Donnacha
couldn't open his mouth. I had his arm, wet
with sweat or maybe it was my own.
The Guard's face on me, wide as a wheel of cheese
under his peak. The tiles felt as if they were
moving then. Even the potted palm seemed
to shake as he asked me about the races
in Newcastle West & had I ever before
or since seen land as rich as you'd see in
the County of Limerick. & Yes, Yes,
I said. I agreed to things I'd never heard in
my life. He said the Limerick grass was so rich,
it would butter your boots. Yes, Yes, I said
again. Pure ould drivel, he must have had
a right laugh, letting us off out the door.

27.

Donnacha must have cursed me afterwards
although they surely had more fellows on
the roof. They would know all the tricks –
weren't they all ex-IRA themselves?
We whirled out the door, I saw Mrs Hayes's
hands go right up to her face. Donnacha
knew straight away because it was pitch black
on the street. He reared his head up. The whites
of his teeth shone like a piano. The lamps!
They have turned off the streetlamps – first & last
English words I heard him say. He turned left
to two Freestaters with fixed bayonets,
two more on the right. Tiocfaidh ár lá, he said.
Our Day will Come & then a river of
Irish followed, the soldiers were making
a desperate mockery of his dress.
It was awful to witness, every hair
on my body standing stiff to hear it.
Pure tramps, the very lowest of the low,
half of them out of the British army
& into Freestate with them. Out of one
uniform into another.

28.

The following day I had a visit from
the Guard – telling me again he was
from my home county as if I could forget
him & his talk of greasy grass. & that
he had a grá for Limerick people,
which was why I was getting off lightly
with myself. I'll give Mrs Hayes credit.
She must have put in a fierce word for me.
Donnacha was for hanging, jail for Eileen
& Mrs Hayes reserved the resident's lounge
for Guard Connolly & myself so he could
give me his hard warning. He said my name
would be kept out of the business but
they all knew down at the Castle next day.
Mr Smith said there was a terrible smell –
Communism in the office. I got the mail
boat from Kingstown the end of the week.

29.

The worst thing about England was no one forced
you to have anything. I'm not talking about
health matters. If you went into a house,
they asked you did you want a cup of tea
& you said no – Right! they would say to you
& that was the end of it. You were left
with your tongue hanging down to your ankles.
There was no such thing as are you sure?
You weren't pressed. No? Fine. Good luck to you.
You could die of hunger & thirst. I only
got the hang of it when I was going.
& I couldn't find my way round either.
Going into the black underground, coming
out at different holes like a mole, blind
& fierce bewildered. London was depressed,
packed with desperate demobbed soldiers.
I was humiliated. You'd be afraid to open
your mouth. I won't repeat the abuse thrown
at the Irish accent. When Mrs Hayes wrote,
I thought I was being invited home.

30.

I couldn't understand all the secrecy.
I thought Mrs Hayes was asking me back
when she wrote but she said afterwards that
it was a hint to stay away. There's not
a single thing in this life that you can't take
in two opposite ways. Especially with people
like Mrs Hayes ready to swear black is white.
She had written two pages on the subject
of potatoes which I read with my homesick heart
bursting from my blouse. Two bags of Golden
Wonders deposited in her cellar
by a man who nearly passed out taking
them down with the sheer weight of them
& they were balls of flour.
Mrs Hayes only wished that I was there
for them, no one appreciated my food
more than you, Miss Cronin & was that an
invitation or what with my mouth
watering as fast as my eyes?

31.

She wrote about Kilmainham Jail, the women
objectors gathering outside, the usual
Tally Ho of the Cumann Na mBan screeching
& roaring, making a show of themselves,
although she had gone down to see herself.
Two respectable middle-aged women said
the rosary outside the gates, they had chairs
to sit on, brought specially by their sons.
They impressed her of course, the snob she is.
They said that if there wasn't censorship
of the Republicans in the first place
girls wouldn't have been arrested for painting
on walls. Mrs Hayes herself wouldn't excuse them,
she said she could rupture the envelope
with news of the Cumann Na mBan capers.
The respectable women insisted
there was ill treatment of the prisoners
& even though she didn't believe
a word of it, Mrs Hayes worried about
Eileen's cough.

32.

I packed again. Before I left, I bought
myself a gramophone & sat beside
the gas fire, winding it up again – John
McCormack records, thinking of Eileen –
I hear you calling me, you called when the moon
had veiled her light, just before you went from
me into the night. I came, do you remember?
Mrs Hayes read me like a book in broad
daylight. I heard her telling Nelly there
was no fool like an old fool & she said
it in front of me so I would hear it.
There was no sign of Marcel, she said
he died with the loneliness after
Eileen but she wasn't one bit upset.
I wouldn't put it past her to kill him.
She made eyes in the mirror behind me
every day I searching & she knowing
full well where Eileen was. & other days
when I thought that if I had to hear John
McCormack again, I would throw myself
out the window & I would be glad to
feel the black ground thundering to meet me.

33.

To be treated like an old fool. To be kept
in ignorance, to be treated like I was mad,
have faces made behind my back in the mirror.
One night I had enough, started shouting.
If she couldn't tell me where Eileen was,
I'd smash every glass in the place. Control
yourself, pipe down, you've drink taken!
I couldn't believe it when she started
talking then & I was sorry for not
bursting out sooner. According to her,
she was on the verge of directing
me to the Mater Hospital, when I'd
interrupted with my undignified shouts.
She said it was a fright to God Eileen
never took a drop of whiskey. It could have
killed the germs. The germs of consumption that
were Eileen's secret, something desperate
bad for the hotel business.

34.

The hardness of the people that would walk
over you if it affected their pockets.
I would have to close down the whole hotel,
the travellers would be gone as fast as
a burst of gunfire. She said that Eileen
was a hard case herself with her cause &
I said, but did you see how she wouldn't
leave Donnacha in the lurch? Mrs Hayes'
eyes filled up then most unexpected.
She told me that he started out as one
of the Fianna, Countess Markievicz's boys.
& that made both of us cry thinking how
he was so young running messages back then,
wearing his own small uniforms. Not even
eighteen when they swung him. Was that legal?
I still don't know & I am afraid to ask.

35.

I saw her in the ward with her white face
& the two black plaits. Her hair had grown out
in the prison, she had the widow's peak –
her light body barely marking the bed.
A nun with a pink face like a marshmallow
squeezed hard into a white coif stood over
her with the priest & the Blessed Sacraments.
Eileen only spoke of Mrs Donavan
& Flora. Almost as if they were there
beside her, with their faces covered in the white
of an egg & their four vain elbows sitting
in the four halves of lemons whitening them.
It's me, Babe Cronin, I said. Eileen, don't
you know me? Her eyes blackened in her white
face as she spoke, Mrs Donavan taught
me darning & fancy darning. I could
do the Peacock's Eye but all I darned was
men's socks & they were always on the run.

DRAMATIS PERSONAE

Mrs Kathleen (Kitty) Donavan: widowed dressmaker.

Himself: Mrs Donavan's husband, believed to be drowned.

Flora Donavan: Mrs Donavan's daughter.

Eileen Murphy: Mrs Donavan's adopted niece, member of Cumann na mBan.

Mr Bloom: Mrs Donavan's Landlord.

Annabella: The Big House, where Mr Bloom lives.

Mr Barry Sullivan: a solicitor, Flora's employer.

Mrs Hayes: Eileen Murphy's aunt, proprietor of Hayes's Hotel, Dublin

Miss Babe Cronin: former stenographer, live-in guest at Hayes's Hotel

Captain Galway: one of two thousand auxiliary military police officers drafted into Ireland in 1920 to put down the rebellion – also known as auxies, they were ex-army officers.

Tans: the Black & Tans, another division of military police, ex-private soldiers also drafted in to suppress the rebels. Their uniform was a mixture of black police tunics & army khaki.

17th Lancers: soldiers stationed at Mallow Garrison since 1732.

Shinners: the military's nickname for the IRA.

Cumann Na mBan: women's division of the IRA.

Note: All the main characters are fictional, but the story in Part 1 is loosely based on real events which took place in Mallow, County Cork on 28 September 1920. Military reprisals were taken against the town following the shooting of Sergeant Gibbs of the 17th Lancers by the IRA during an arms raid on Mallow Barracks.